Original title:

A Symphony of Dreams

Copyright © 2025 Swan Charm

All rights reserved.

Author: Mirell Mesipuu

ISBN HARDBACK: 978-9908-1-4813-7

ISBN PAPERBACK: 978-9908-1-4814-4

ISBN EBOOK: 978-9908-1-4815-1

Harmonizing Fantasies with Reality

In the quiet of the night, dreams take flight,
Whispers of wishes dance in soft moonlight.
Stars above weave tales so bright,
Capturing hearts in a sweet delight.

Yet dawn breaks with its golden gleam,
Reality stirs, shaking the dream.
Promises made in a silken stream,
Fading away like a distant beam.

In between worlds, we find our place,
Balancing hope with a tender grace.
With each heartbeat, we embrace the chase,
Merging two realms in a warm embrace.

Mountains of passion rise and fall,
Echoing softly, they call, they call.
In the tapestry woven, we stand tall,
Finding our strength, ready to sprawl.

A symphony calls from the depths inside,
Where dreams and truth in harmony glide.
Together they thrive, never to hide,
In this beautiful dance, forever allied.

Echoes of Twilight Whispers

In the dusk, shadows play,
Softly fading light of day,
Whispers in the evening air,
Secrets longing to be shared.

Stars appear, a gentle glow,
Casting dreams, where rivers flow,
Echoes of a night so deep,
Where the silent moments keep.

Melodies in the Moonlight

Lunar beams caress the night,
Softly weaving threads of light,
Underneath the silver skies,
Melodies where silence lies.

Hearts align with every tune,
Dancing softly under moon,
Notes like whispers in the breeze,
Carried forth with quiet ease.

Harmony of Wandering Thoughts

Thoughts like rivers drift away,
In the stillness, they will play,
Flowing freely, seeking peace,
In their depths, a sweet release.

Caught between the heart and mind,
In the echoes, truth we find,
A harmony of whispered dreams,
Where nothing's truly as it seems.

Crescendo of Enchanted Visions

Visions dance in twilight's realm,
Where shadows rise, but light can helm,
Crescendo building, soft and sweet,
In the silence, hear the beat.

Each moment, like a fleeting sigh,
Colors blend as night draws nigh,
Enchanted paths before our eyes,
Leading forth to starlit skies.

Illuminated Paths of Intent

In the dawn's embrace, we walk,
With every step, our spirits talk.
Dreams unfold in golden rays,
Guiding us through life's maze.

Stars above begin to weave,
Stories of the hearts that grieve.
Intentions clear, like morning dew,
A chance to start life anew.

With every choice, a light we spark,
In shadows deep, we leave a mark.
Paths illuminated, choices bright,
Forging truth within the night.

Together we dance, hand in hand,
Creating hope in a vast land.
With kindness as our steady guide,
We'll find our way, and not divide.

The Art of Dreamscapes

In twilight's breath, our visions bloom,
Crafted softly in the room.
Brushstrokes of silence paint the air,
Awakening wishes gathered with care.

Colors blend where thoughts entwine,
Shaping realms, a space divine.
Through whispers of the night's embrace,
We wander free in this dreamscape place.

Each canvas holds a hidden truth,
Unveiling visions of eternal youth.
In every heartbeat, stories grow,
A journey deep where dreams can flow.

With every sigh, creation starts,
Connecting souls from distant parts.
The art of dreams, a sacred start,
Encapsulating the dreaming heart.

Veils of the Imagination

Beneath the layers, secrets hide,
In whispers low, where dreams reside.
Veils of thought, like gossamer wings,
Carrying tales that the heart sings.

Through shimmers soft, we travel far,
Chasing visions, a distant star.
Each layer peeled reveals a sight,
A world where darkness meets the light.

In playful hues, the mind expands,
Creating wonders with gentle hands.
Imagination's dance, bright and free,
Awakens realms for all to see.

Through the veil, the dreams unfold,
Stories waiting to be told.
In this realm, our spirits soar,
Finding magic forevermore.

Whimsical Whispers of Fate

In gardens where the wildflowers sway,
Whispers of fate gently play.
Each breeze carries stories untold,
Of dreams once lost and wishes bold.

The sun dips low, painting the skies,
As laughter dances, and hope arises.
With every petal, a promise made,
In whimsical moments, we find our trade.

Time twirls softly in a gentle waltz,
Reminding us of life's sweet faults.
With heartbeats echoing the song,
In each whisper, we all belong.

Fate's brush strokes paint our days,
In vibrant colors, in myriad ways.
Embracing chance, we find our fate,
In whimsical whispers, love awaits.

Cadence of the Celestial

Stars twinkle in night's embrace,
Whispers of the cosmic grace.
Galaxies swirl in silent song,
Time flows where we all belong.

Nebulas paint the dark with light,
Echoes of our dreams take flight.
Celestial bodies dance and play,
Guiding our hearts on the way.

Wings of Imagination

On feathered dreams, we take our flight,
Across the canvas of the night.
Each stroke a tale that comes alive,
In realms where hopes and wishes thrive.

We soar on breezes of delight,
Through clouds that shimmer, soft and bright.
In visions born from whispered prayer,
The world unfolds, vibrant and rare.

Unfurled

Petals burst from buds with grace,
In a dance of time and space.
Unfurled dreams in morning's glow,
Nature's beauty starts to flow.

Colors blend, a fragrant blend,
A symphony that will not end.
Every leaf, a whispered cheer,
Telling tales we long to hear.

Tuning Forks of the Heart

In stillness, listen to the sound,
Where echoes of our souls are found.
Tuning forks strike the deepest part,
Resonating from the heart.

Each note, a memory, a sigh,
Floating softly, never shy.
Together in the quiet night,
We find the harmony of light.

The Dreamcatcher's Waltz

Webs spun with threads of silver hue,
Catch the dreams that bid adieu.
Hopes entwined in every strand,
Guided gently by fate's hand.

In the night, they sway and dance,
Lifting spirits in a trance.
Each flutter tells a tale anew,
In the waltz of dreams, we pursue.

Tides of Imagination

Waves whisper soft dreams,
Carrying thoughts on their swell.
Colors dance in the air,
Painting stories to tell.

Shadows merge with the light,
Creating worlds of delight.
Hearts flutter with each tide,
Lost in the magic of night.

Every crest holds a wish,
Daring the stars to collide.
In this ocean of thought,
We drift where hopes abide.

Time flows like the sea,
Endless and vast in its grace.
In this realm of the mind,
We find our sacred space.

With each ebb and each flow,
Imagination takes flight.
Riding the currents of dreams,
We soar into the night.

Nocturnal Serenades

Moonlight bathes the ground,
Casting shadows so deep.
Crickets chirp their sweet songs,
Enchanting the world as we sleep.

Stars twinkle like diamonds,
In a velvet sky so grand.
Whispers of gentle breezes,
Caress the slumbering land.

Dreamers lay lost in thought,
As night drapes its soft cloak.
Hearts beat to the silence,
In harmony, they evoke.

Each breath a melody,
In the stillness profound.
Nocturnal serenades play,
In the solace we've found.

With each passing moment,
Time lingers with grace.
Nocturnal symphonies call,
To our tranquil embrace.

Fantasies in Flight

Wings spread wide in the breeze,
Chasing the sun's warm rays.
Clouds become our playground,
In this world where we stay.

Tiny whispers of joy,
Dancing on currents of air.
Dreams blossom like flowers,
In a realm without care.

Every heartbeat a soaring,
In the sky, we roam free.
Fantasies take to the heavens,
Like birds wild and carefree.

With each flicker of hope,
We rise on the wings of fate.
Lost in this playful wonder,
We'll never be late.

In the tapestry of dreams,
Life paints its vibrant hues.
Fantasies in flight,
Are the moments we choose.

Reveries Under the Silver Sky

Glistening night unfolds,
Silver threads weave the dark.
Echoes of whispers float,
Illuminating the stark.

Stars tell tales from afar,
Stories of love and fate.
Underneath the vast canvas,
We dream and we create.

Moonbeams dance on the lake,
Reflecting our silent sighs.
In the stillness we linger,
Boundless as night skies.

With every breath of the night,
Hope drifts upon a sigh.
Reveries in the quiet,
Beneath the silver sky.

Magic swirls in the air,
In this cherished embrace.
Through the veil of our dreams,
We find our sacred space.

Kaleidoscope of Illusions

Colors dance and swirl anew,
Fragments caught in twisted views,
Dreams unfold beneath the light,
Reality fades into the night.

Shapes that twist in vibrant hues,
Echoes of forgotten muse,
Every turn a vision bold,
Stories whispered, yet untold.

Mirrors shatter with a glance,
Life a fleeting, fickle dance,
In this world of shifting seams,
Lost within our fractured dreams.

Patterns weave a silent song,
Where the heart can't help but long,
For a truth that slips away,
In a game we seldom play.

Caught within this broken sphere,
Chasing shadows, holding fear,
Yet in chaos, beauty lies,
In the kaleidoscope of skies.

The Soundtrack of Lost Moments

Silent echoes fill the air,
Notes of life too sweet to bear,
Every laugh and whispered sigh,
Fleeting memories passing by.

In this symphony of time,
Chords of joy and pain entwined,
Each heartbeat plays a different tune,
Woven deep in afternoon.

Faded photographs refrain,
Melodies that sound like rain,
In the hush of twilight's glow,
We remember what we know.

Drifting voices softly blend,
Each refrain a cherished friend,
As the world begins to fade,
In the silence, dreams are made.

But within this gentle strife,
Songs will echo, hint of life,
A collection of sweet love's art,
The soundtrack etched upon the heart.

Rhapsody of the Unconscious

Dive into the depths unseen,
Where shadows dance in shades of green,
Thoughts that spin like autumn leaves,
In the web the mind conceives.

Streaming whispers, secrets flow,
In soft currents, ebb and glow,
Silent rhapsody of dreams,
Echoes caught in mental streams.

Voices linger, fleeting grace,
Searching for a sacred space,
In the labyrinth beneath,
Where the heart and dreamers breathe.

Listen closely, hear the sighs,
Wonders tucked in soft goodbyes,
Memories like fireflies spark,
Guiding pathways through the dark.

In this canvas stretched so wide,
Inner realms we cannot hide,
Find the beauty deep within,
In the rhapsody begin.

Whirlwinds of Whimsy

Spin with me in playful glee,
Round and round, just you and me,
Colors blend and laughter flies,
In this world of sweet surprise.

Silly thoughts like petals bloom,
Dancing in a sunlit room,
Joyful chaos, blissful turns,
Heart alight with vibrant burns.

Chasing dreams on whimsy's wings,
One little gust, a thousand things,
Twirling through the morning mist,
Every moment, life kissed.

In each nudge and gentle spin,
Letting go, the fun begins,
Spiraling through the bright unknown,
In this whirlwind, love has grown.

So let the winds of laughter blow,
Through fields of joy where wildflowers grow,
For in this whimsy, we find the key,
To the magic of being free.

Cascading Echoes of the Mind

Thoughts like rivers gently flow,
In hidden depths where shadows grow.
Whispers blend in twilight's grace,
Cascading echoes find their place.

Silent dreams take flight at night,
In realms beyond the morning light.
A symphony of voices calls,
As consciousness and memory thralls.

Rippling visions, fleeting fast,
Fragments of a distant past.
Each moment captured, yet escapes,
In currents where the stillness shapes.

Minds collide like stars on high,
Creating constellations nigh.
Patterns weave a tapestry grand,
In the quiet where thoughts expand.

Within the ebb and flow of time,
We find our rhythms, our own rhyme.
Cascading echoes softly chime,
In the corridors of the mind.

The Quietude of Wonder

In the stillness, secrets bloom,
Each heartbeat stirs the silent gloom.
Nature whispers soft and low,
In quietude, the heart will grow.

Stars above in velvet skies,
Sparkle like forgotten sighs.
Innocence wraps the night in lace,
As time reveals each hidden face.

Curious souls in shadows dance,
Embracing life's enchanting chance.
Moments held in gentle sway,
In awe of what the night can say.

Beneath the moon's soft, tender gaze,
We lose ourselves in silent praise.
Every breath, a fleeting spark,
Igniting dreams within the dark.

The quietude unveils each thought,
In reverie, we find what's sought.
With open hearts, we dare to see,
The wonder that will always be.

Chronicles of the Unseen

In shadows deep, where stories hide,
The chronicles of time abide.
Threads of fate in silence weave,
Unseen tales we dare believe.

In twilight's hush, the past draws near,
Echoes linger, crystal clear.
Voices from an ancient place,
In whispered tones, they leave a trace.

Through veils of mist and woven dreams,
Reality isn't what it seems.
Lost in tales of yesteryear,
Each moment whispers, loud and clear.

The unseen paths we often tread,
Guide us where the brave have led.
With every step, a story starts,
Penned in the chambers of our hearts.

Chronicles dance just out of sight,
Illuminating day and night.
In the depths, their wisdom gleans,
Revealing life's mysterious scenes.

Threads of Light and Shadow

In the tapestry of life we weave,
Threads of light and shadow cleave.
Moments blend in colors bright,
A dance of joy, a touch of fright.

Each heartbeat paints a story true,
In shades of gold and deepest blue.
Upon this canvas, dreams align,
A shimmer where the stars entwine.

Cascades of laughter, echoes sound,
In every corner, love is found.
Yet shadows linger, soft and sweet,
In every loss, we feel complete.

The duality of joy and pain,
A gentle storm, a tender rain.
Through contrasts, life begins to show,
The beauty in the ebb and flow.

Threads of light beneath the skin,
Binding stories deep within.
In the quiet, shadows rest,
A symphony that feels the best.

Whispers of Stardust

In the quiet of the night,
Stars dance upon the sky.
Each whispering spark a tale,
Of dreams that never die.

Soft glimmers light the dark,
Like secrets on the breeze.
They twinkle, weave, and play,
In cosmic melodies.

Beneath the velvet dome,
We trace our hopes so high.
In stardust trails we roam,
As silent wishes fly.

The universe expands,
With every breath we take.
In that vastness, we find,
The dreams we dare to make.

So gather 'round the night,
Let stardust guide our way.
For in the whispers deep,
A spark can light the day.

Melodies in the Moonlight

Serenading shadowed trees,
The moon sings soft and clear.
Notes drift like gentle winds,
Filling the heart with cheer.

Silver beams cascade down,
As night embraces all.
Every rustle in the leaves,
Is nature's sweet enthrall.

In the dance of misty nights,
We find a rhythm true.
Harmonies with stars align,
As dreams begin anew.

The world pauses to listen,
To a song from afar.
In moonlit symphony,
We find our guiding star.

So let the night unfold,
With its whispers low and sweet.
In the melodies of light,
Our hearts and dreams compete.

Echoes of Enchanted Visions

In forests deep and wild,
Where shadows softly play,
The echoes call us closer,
To dreams that softly sway.

With every rustle, whispers,
A magic stirs the air.
The echoes spin their tales,
Of secrets hidden there.

Through twilight's gentle veil,
Visions dance like sighs.
In that realm of wonders,
Our spirits learn to fly.

What stories lie unspoken,
In silence held so tight?
The echoes of our heartbeats,
Join in the dance of night.

So linger here a moment,
Let visions intertwine.
For in this sacred silence,
Our souls begin to shine.

Serenade of the Sleepwalker

In the stillness of the night,
A wanderer takes flight.
With steps of softest whispers,
Through shadows dim and light.

He weaves a path of dreams,
With starlit eyes aglow.
Each twinkle is a secret,
That only he can know.

Across the azure skies,
His heart begins to soar.
In slumber's sweet embrace,
He seeks forevermore.

Their serenade a melody,
That echoes through the night.
With every whispered step,
He dances, pure delight.

An ethereal connection,
To worlds both far and wide.
A sleepwalker's bold journey,
With dreams he cannot hide.

Hallways of Hypnotic Hues

In twilight whispers, colors blend,
A journey starts, where visions bend.
Echoes of soft, enchanting light,
Drawn deeper still, into the night.

Painted walls of thoughts untold,
Whirling tales of hues so bold.
A lull of time, a sweet adrift,
In corridors where dreams are sift.

Fingers brush the edges fine,
In sacred halls, where shadows twine.
Spectrum dances, fluid grace,
Finding solace in this space.

Each step forward, heartbeats race,
Memories dip in vibrant lace.
A ribboned path, of twists and turns,
In hypnotic hues, the spirit yearns.

So wander deep through realms sublime,
In every shade, in thoughts that rhyme.
For here in stillness, all renew,
In hallways rich with hypnotic hue.

The Croon of the Cosmos

Beneath the stars, a lullaby,
Soft whispers from the endless sky.
Galaxies sing in cosmic swell,
A gentle tune, a mystic spell.

Celestial notes in velvet dark,
Each tone a spark, each note a mark.
Swaying planets in harmony,
Revealing secrets, wild and free.

Time unfurls in gentle waves,
As stardust twinkles, the heart braves.
In the hush, the universe breathes,
A symphony that never leaves.

The moonlight spreads its silver lace,
As dreams take flight through boundless space.
Awake, I hear that tender croon,
The cosmos' heart, a timeless tune.

So bask in melodies divine,
Embrace the night, let lights align.
For in the quiet, we find our place,
In the croon of the cosmos, our embrace.

Lullabies from the Abyss

In depths unseen, where shadows wave,
The water sings, a haunting grave.
An ancient song of sorrow's plight,
Lulls the weary through the night.

Echoes drift on icy streams,
Cradling lost and shattered dreams.
Beneath the waves, the silence feels,
A soft embrace that gently heals.

Hidden realms, where phantoms play,
Their lullabies can't fade away.
With every note, the darkness sways,
Navigating through the shadowed maze.

A tender pull from depths profound,
Each whispered word, a solemn sound.
For those who seek the calm abyss,
Find peace within the silent kiss.

So listen close to what's untold,
In lullabies that brave and bold.
For in the depths, the heart takes flight,
In lullabies from the abyss, pure night.

Shadows Dancing with Dreams

In the twilight's gentle sway,
Shadows spin in grand ballet.
Whispers twirl upon the floor,
Embracing dreams forevermore.

Figures twine in silent grace,
Lost inside this mystic space.
Stars above weave silver streams,
While shadows dance with hidden dreams.

Echoed laughter fills the air,
In a waltz that banishes despair.
The nighttime's magic pulses bright,
As dreams and shadows take their flight.

Beneath the moon, a tender glow,
The heartbeats rise; the visions flow.
In each soft step, the night unveils,
A dance of hope where spirit sails.

So take my hand, let's drift away,
Where shadows blend with dreams at play.
In this embrace, we come alive,
In shadows dancing, our souls thrive.

Celestial Rhythms

In the night sky's vast embrace,
Stars pulse with gentle grace.
Whispers of cosmic lore,
Echo through the universe's core.

Planets twirl in silent glee,
Ballet of eternity.
Galaxies spin like a dream,
In the starlit silver stream.

Pulsars utter rhythmic sound,
In harmony, they are found.
Nebulas paint the sky wide,
With colors that never hide.

Time dances in stardust's glow,
A celestial stage for all to know.
Life's questions, they unfold,
In the tales that light years hold.

Eternity sways, a mystic band,
In the cosmos, hand in hand.
Celestial rhythms, soft and deep,
In the night sky's dreamless sleep.

Dances Among the Distant Stars

Beneath a veil of midnight blue,
Stars perform for me and you.
Graceful orbits, twinkling lights,
In the silence of the nights.

Comets streak, a fleeting glance,
Galactic waltz, a timeless dance.
Cosmic rhythms intertwine,
In the heavens, souls align.

Planets spin in distant dreams,
Rippling through the starlit beams.
Sirius shines, a beacon bright,
Guiding wishes into the night.

From shadowed realms to brightened skies,
The universe swells, gently sighs.
In the vast, where wonders twirl,
Dances weave, and visions whirl.

Every twinkle holds a tale,
Of cosmic love that will not fail.
Join the dance, let spirits soar,
Among the stars forevermore.

Dreams Adrift on Gossamer Wings

In the twilight's soft embrace,
Dreams unfold in gentle grace.
Gossamer wings take to flight,
Whispers wrapped in starlight.

Through the clouds, hopes arise,
Chasing shadows, touching skies.
Each flutter, a fleeting chance,
In the quiet night's romance.

Murmurs of worlds never seen,
Echo softly, sharp and keen.
On the breeze, our wishes sway,
Guiding adventurers on their way.

Time drifts like a feathered dream,
In a world more fragile than it seems.
Lost in thoughts of realms unknown,
Together where we have grown.

Every dream, a spark of light,
Carried through the velvet night.
Adrift on wings so fragile, true,
Chasing wonders, me and you.

The Enchantment of Forgotten Thoughts

In the corners of our minds,
Soft whispers of the past unwind.
Memories dance, a ghostly trace,
Fleeting smiles, a sweet embrace.

Thoughts like shadows, linger low,
In the twilight, soft and slow.
Echoes of laughter, lost in time,
Resonate in whispered rhyme.

Pages turning, stories fold,
In the heart, treasures untold.
Visions bloom, like flowers rare,
Fragrant dreams fill the air.

Magic lives in moments gone,
In the quiet, dusk to dawn.
Awakening through gentle light,
Forgotten thoughts, take flight.

Through the haze, a glimpse we find,
Of love and loss, intertwined.
The enchantment we hold so dear,
In the whispers of the years.

Lullabies of Cosmic Journeys

In the hush of night, stars softly gleam,
Whispers of the void, a celestial dream.
Cradled in the arms of the endless vast,
Waves of time drift by, the future and past.

Galaxies swirl in a cosmic waltz,
Carrying secrets, the universe halts.
Floating through shadows, soft stardust flows,
Guiding the lost on where starlight goes.

Moonbeams caress, as light takes its flight,
Sailing through the depths of the shimmering night.
Embers of hope in the silent expanse,
Cradle the weary, invite them to dance.

Nebulae sigh, as dreams start to spin,
Weaving the fabric where journeys begin.
Breathe in the cosmos, embrace the unknown,
For in every heartbeat, a universe grown.

Hearts full of wonder, ignite the spark,
In the lullabies sung by the void and the dark.
Close your eyes gently, let the stars guide,
In this tranquil symphony, we drift and reside.

Chords of Starlit Longing

In the vast expanse, a melody rings,
Chords of the cosmos, frail voices sing.
Echoes of longing drift through the night,
Tales of adventures beneath starlit light.

Across the firmament, currents entwine,
Whispering secrets, both yours and mine.
Harmony of destinies, paths intertwine,
In the tapestry woven, your hand in mine.

The moonlight dances, casting its glow,
Lighting the trails where old memories flow.
Yearning for moments that never took shape,
In the silence of night, where dreams softly drape.

With every heartbeat, a story unfolds,
A tune of the ages, brave and bold.
Resonating softly in the heart of the sea,
Where waves of love carry you back to me.

So let us wander through this serenade,
In the embrace of starlight, fears start to fade.
With every note sung, our spirits align,
In the chords of longing, our souls truly shine.

Rhythms of the Unseen Realm

In shadows and whispers, a pulse you can trace,
Rhythms of the unseen, an endless embrace.
Dancing on edges where silence takes form,
Through the veil of the night, our spirits transform.

Echoes of heartbeat, a cadence of life,
Interwoven stories of peace and of strife.
Where echoes converge, unseen forces play,
Guiding the dreamers who wander astray.

Through corridors woven in threads of the dark,
We find the soft glow, the elusive spark.
In the gentle cadence, the unseen thrives,
Resonating softly, where the mystery lives.

Unfolding like petals in the moonlit haze,
The dance of existence ignites the gaze.
Heartbeat in stillness, a rhythm we share,
In the realm of the unknown, stripped bare.

Together we venture through worlds intertwined,
Exploring the depths where true magic is blind.
With every heartbeat, a question untold,
In the rhythms of life, our stories unfold.

Serenade of the Dreamweaver

In the twilight glow, where dreams start to sway,
The dreamweaver whispers, guiding the way.
Stitches of starlight in the fabric of night,
Embroidery of visions, a world taking flight.

With every soft sigh, a new tale is spun,
Woven with laughter, the rising of sun.
A dance of the mind, where shadows dissolve,
In the heart of the dream, we endlessly revolve.

Carried by breezes of shimmering hope,
The dreamweaver beckons, inviting to cope.
Through valleys of whispers where wishes can bloom,
Awakening treasures concealed in the gloom.

Moonbeams cast light on the pathways we trace,
Chasing the echoes, embracing our grace.
In the soft serenade of visions we find,
The beauty of dreaming, unchained and unblind.

With threads of imagination, we weave our delight,
In the embrace of creation, hearts take to flight.
So listen intently, as stars serenade,
In the world of the dreamer, magic won't fade.

Echoing Footsteps in Slumber

In the stillness of night, they tread,
Whispers of dreams softly spread.
Shadows dance on the edge of sight,
Carrying secrets from day to night.

Gentle hearts in twilight's embrace,
Floating softly in a serene space.
With each echo, the memories call,
Binding the silence, enchanting all.

A symphony composed, quiet yet loud,
Lost within the slumbering crowd.
Footsteps trace paths in the moon's soft glow,
Guiding the dreams where wishes flow.

In slumber's hold, time drifts away,
Beneath the stars, where we long to stay.
Each echo a note in the lullaby's hymn,
Playing the tune of life's secret whim.

So let the footsteps lead us deep,
Into the realms where the lost dreams sleep.
In this night's embrace, we shall find,
The echo of whispers, gentle and kind.

Cadence of Limitless Horizons

Upon the edge of the vast unknown,
Waves of adventure eagerly grown.
With each sunrise, the promise unfolds,
A symphony sung in colors bold.

The journey calls, a siren's plea,
Where horizons blend with the endless sea.
Each step forward, a heartbeat's dance,
Awakening dreams that dare to chance.

Skyward we look, as the world expands,
Carving our fate with open hands.
The cadence of life, a vibrant thread,
Stitching the stories that lie ahead.

Limitless whispers in the winds of fate,
Guiding our souls, as we navigate.
In every heartbeat, the universe spins,
Embracing the depths where our journey begins.

Together we wander, hearts intertwined,
Chasing horizons, so far yet aligned.
In the rhythm of existence, we find our place,
A cadence of life that we shall embrace.

Rhapsody of Uncharted Minds

In the theater of thoughts unbound,
Ideas bloom where silence is found.
A rhapsody sung in whispers and sighs,
Painting the canvas where imagination flies.

Through the corridors of dreams we weave,
Crafting the tales that we dare to believe.
Every spark ignites a vision's flight,
A symphony echoing through the night.

Thoughts like rivers flow wild and free,
Breaking the limits of what we can see.
Uncharted minds in a vast expanse,
Dancing with shadows in a daring trance.

The melodies swirl in a cosmic embrace,
Fueling the passion that time won't erase.
In the rhapsody, we discover our truth,
As fragments of memory recall our youth.

From the depths of silence, we boldly rise,
Chasing the wonders beneath endless skies.
Together we dream in the melody's flow,
A rhapsody of life that continues to grow.

Fugue of Unspoken Desires

In the hush of night, desires murmur,
Softly echoing like whispers of fervor.
A fugue of thoughts, hidden from view,
Crafting a melody both ancient and new.

Emotions entwined in delicate threads,
Carving the silence where courage treads.
Each heartbeat reveals a longing untold,
A dance of shadows, tender and bold.

Under the stars, where secrets reside,
The pulse of dreams cannot be denied.
With every glance, a story unfolds,
In the quietude, our truth beholds.

Yearnings alive, in a passionate swirl,
A tapestry woven, as worlds unfurl.
In the fugue, we find our desire's spark,
Illuminating paths through the endless dark.

So let the unspoken take flight tonight,
Guiding our souls to the realms of light.
In the fugue of longing, we find our way,
Dancing with hopes that refuse to sway.

Serenades of the Infinite

In twilight's hush, we find our song,
A melody that lingers long.
Stars whisper secrets in the night,
We dance to dreams, a pure delight.

The cosmos cradles every note,
Our hearts alight, they gently float.
Through endless skies, our spirits soar,
Each serenade inspires more.

Time bends with harmonies so sweet,
In every pulse, our souls complete.
Together woven, hand in hand,
We traverse this ethereal land.

Beneath the vault of twinkling eyes,
We shed our fears, we grow the ties.
The universe, a symphony,
In every breath, infinity.

So raise your voice, let echoes weave,
In this vast world, we believe.
For in the night, love's serenade,
Will guide our hearts, never to fade.

Sculpting Dreams in the Ether

With hands of hope, we carve the air,
Molding visions with utmost care.
In twilight's glow, where whispers play,
We shape our dreams, come what may.

Each thought a stone, we chip away,
Creating paths where shadows lay.
The ether hums with vibrant light,
As we sculpt futures, bold and bright.

In the silence, inspiration flows,
From deep within, our passion grows.
Crafting realms where courage reigns,
With every heartbeat, love remains.

As stars are born from cosmic dust,
We forge our truths, in hope we trust.
In artistry, our spirits dance,
In dreams unleashed, we find our chance.

So let us dream with open hearts,
In every breath, a brand new start.
Through the ether, our dreams extend,
Together, we create, we mend.

Reflections on a Moonbeam

Upon the lake, a silver thread,
Moonlight whispers where dreams are led.
In gentle waves, our thoughts collide,
As night unveils what hearts confide.

Beneath the glow, we float in peace,
Our fears and doubts begin to cease.
With every ripple, secrets shared,
In moonlit grace, our souls are bared.

The darkness lifts, revealing bright,
A world aglow, bathed in light.
We chase the spark of fleeting dreams,
In this embrace, nothing's as it seems.

Reflections dance, like stars they weave,
A tapestry of what we believe.
With open eyes, our hearts align,
In moonbeams' glow, our spirits shine.

So linger here, in starlit hue,
As night bestows its magic new.
In tranquil waters, love cascades,
Reflections pure, time gently fades.

The Prelude of Possibility

At dawn's first light, a promise births,
A canvas blank, where hope finds worth.
In every shade, the future gleams,
Awakening the brightest dreams.

With open hearts, we greet the day,
Creating paths along the way.
The air is thick with what could be,
Unfolding like a mystery.

In moments shared, we break the mold,
As stories wait, yet to be told.
The world a stage, our roles unwind,
In every glance, new worlds we find.

The whispers of the wind implore,
To leap beyond the closed-off door.
We dance to themes of what's ahead,
In every heartbeat, dreams are spread.

So take a breath, embrace the now,
With courage, we'll learn just how.
For in this prelude, life unfolds,
A symphony of dreams retold.

Vignettes of a Dreamweaver

In twilight's gentle grasp, dreams arise,
Colors swirl beneath the hazy skies.
Whispers of wishes float in the night,
As shadows dance in soft, fleeting light.

A tapestry woven of hopes and fears,
Grasping the echoes of forgotten years.
Silhouettes drift on the edge of pure thought,
In this realm, all is cherished and sought.

Threads of silver glimmer in the dark,
Each moment captured, a timeless spark.
Visions flicker like stars up above,
In the palaces built of dreams and love.

With each heartbeat, a story unfolds,
A map of the heart, in silence it holds.
The weaver spins tales of joy and despair,
In the quiet, we linger, lost in the air.

So dream on, travelers, beneath the veil,
For in every ending, a new tale will sail.
The night is a canvas, vast and profound,
In the art of dreaming, true magic is found.

Ruminations Under the Stars

Under the vastness of a shimmering sky,
Thoughts meander like clouds drifting high.
Each star a question, a whisper of light,
Illuminating the depths of the night.

Beneath the cosmos, old tales intertwine,
Stories of hearts beating in rhythm divine.
Reflections cascade like a soft summer's breeze,
In the silence, the mind finds its ease.

Every twinkle a promise of dreams yet to come,
The world feels undone, soft and so numb.
In the celestial gaze, the soul finds its place,
A heartbeat of wonder in the infinite space.

As the moon weaves its silver across the morn,
Hope blossoms gently with each new dawn.
Ruminating softly, we weave our own tales,
With starlit whispers that dance and unveil.

So gather your thoughts, let them soar and fly,
In the expanse of wonder, the heart learns to sigh.
For beneath the stars, we are all intertwined,
In the beauty of ruminations, dreams aligned.

Flutters of a Fleeting Thought

A fluttering whisper passes through the air,
A thought takes flight, light as a prayer.
Moments of clarity, brief and divine,
Like fireflies caught in the weave of time.

In a blink of an eye, the world can fade,
Lost in the wonders we silently made.
Crystalline visions dance on the breeze,
Fleeting reflections that come and then cease.

Glances exchanged in the softest light,
Promises linger, though shadows ignite.
A flicker of time, so precious yet quick,
Moments slip past as we try to keep thick.

Yet in every flutter, a heartbeat remains,
A tapestry woven of joys and of pains.
Captured in whispers, like petals in flight,
Fleeting thoughts linger, holding on tight.

So cherish the moments, both dim and bright,
For each fleeting thought is a beacon of light.
In the flutters of being, the essence is found,
Life's intricate dance, eternally bound.

The Language of Fantasies

In the realm of dreams, where shadows reside,
Fantasies bloom, drawing hearts to confide.
A dialect spoken in colors and light,
Unraveling secrets that glimmer at night.

Every whisper unfolds a story untold,
In the garden of wishes where desires mold.
The heart learns to listen, to feel, and to see,
In the dance of the soul, wild and free.

Characters twirl in a symphony bright,
Painting the canvas of endless delight.
With brushes of laughter and strokes of despair,
The language of fantasies hangs in the air.

Through valleys of longing and peaks of desire,
We chase the elixirs that set us on fire.
For behind every smile, a fantasy lies,
Waiting to soar, to sparkle, and rise.

So listen with wonder, let your heart sway,
In the language of dreams, find your way.
For every heartbeat is a symphony grand,
In the world of fantasies, together we stand.

Harmonics of the Heart

In whispers soft, the heart does sing,
A melody of joy, a gentle ring.
With every pulse, a story spun,
In chords of love, our souls have won.

A dance of dreams beneath the sky,
Echoes of laughter, moments fly.
Each beat a promise, pure and true,
Together, dear, I live for you.

The strum of fate in twilight's glow,
Notes intertwine, as rivers flow.
In shadows cast by starlit grace,
Harmonies bloom in love's embrace.

With every sigh, the world aligns,
In the symphony of our designs.
Through highs and lows, in joyful art,
We weave the magic of the heart.

So let the music guide our way,
Through night to dawn, in love's ballet.
In every heartbeat, in every start,
Resounds the song of the heart.

Nightfall's Lullaby

The stars awaken, a gentle sigh,
As shadows stretch, the night draws nigh.
Crickets sing their soft refrain,
In dusk's embrace, we feel no pain.

Moonlight dances on the grass,
Whispers secrets, as moments pass.
Clouds drift softly, dreams take flight,
Wrapped in peace, we greet the night.

Each star a wish, a hope, a dream,
The world asleep, in silver gleam.
In tender silence, hearts align,
As night unfolds, our souls entwine.

With every breath, the night weaves deep,
A soothing lull, in dreams we leap.
Embraced by shadows, we drift away,
Into the magic of night's ballet.

In this stillness, fears take flight,
Nestled safe in the arms of night.
As slumber's kiss begins to flow,
We find our peace in nightfall's glow.

Chasing Shadows in the Twilight

In the hush of dusk, shadows play,
Chasing whispers, drifting away.
Colors blend in a soft embrace,
Moments linger, time slows its pace.

The horizon glows, a canvas bright,
Where day surrenders to the night.
Footsteps echo on the quiet lane,
In twilight's arms, we feel no pain.

Laughter mingles with fading light,
Secrets shared in the warm twilight.
Every shadow conceals a tale,
As dreams begin to set their sail.

With hope ignited, we dance with grace,
In the soft shadows, we find our place.
Chasing memories whispered low,
As twilight casts its ethereal glow.

So let us wander, hearts aligned,
Through this journey, love defined.
In chasing shadows, we've found our way,
As night unfolds, we embrace the play.

The Canvas of Reveries

With every stroke, the colors blend,
A tapestry where dreams transcend.
In shades of hope and whispers bright,
We paint our wishes under the light.

The canvas waits for tales untold,
In vibrant hues, our hearts unfold.
Each brush a heartbeat, every line,
A story woven, pure and divine.

Imagination soars, wild and free,
Creating worlds for you and me.
In every layer, secrets hide,
In this canvas, our souls collide.

With every hue, a heartbeat shared,
In this masterpiece, love is declared.
As colors dance, and passions ignite,
We find our truth in pure delight.

So let us dream on this canvas vast,
In strokes of joy, our shadows cast.
In the realm of reveries, we shall roam,
Painting our visions, creating our home.

Nocturne of Fantastical Realities

In shadows deep where wishes blend,
Whispers of dreams begin to send.
Stars like lanterns softly gleam,
Awakening the haunted dream.

Through realms unseen our spirits fly,
Chasing the echoes of a sigh.
Each heartbeat marks a secret choice,
In the silence, hear the voice.

Beneath the moon's enchanting light,
We wander through the velvet night.
Each step a dance, a fleeting chance,
In this ethereal, endless trance.

The tapestry of night unfolds,
With tales of love and dreams retold.
In the cradle of the universe,
We find our truth, we're free to traverse.

So let us revel in the night,
Where fantasies take wondrous flight.
In the nocturne's gentle sway,
We'll cherish dreams that softly play.

Ballad of the Heart's Reverie

In quiet moments, whispers flow,
The heart reveals what we must know.
With every beat, a story spun,
A dance of souls, two minds as one.

Through tangled paths and gentle sighs,
Love's melody forever lies.
A serenade to dreams we share,
In starlit nights, in open air.

Each glance a spark, a silent plea,
The world fades out, just you and me.
In echoes sweet, our laughter rings,
Together we write what the heart sings.

Through trials faced and joys embraced,
In every memory, love's traced.
A symphony, a tender theme,
In the garden of our dream.

So hold my hand, let's chase the dawn,
With every heartbeat, we press on.
In the ballad of our tender art,
Forever shall we never part.

Aria of Fleeting Moments

In fleeting seconds, time does play,
With whispered winds that drift away.
Each heartbeat holds a precious key,
Unlocking dreams of you and me.

The sunlight dances on the stream,
Reflecting hopes that softly gleam.
A fragile touch, a shared embrace,
In moments lost, we find our place.

As petals fall, so do we sigh,
For every breath, a goodbye nigh.
Yet in the whispers of the breeze,
Our laughter lingers, soft like leaves.

Each blink a snapshot, time does bend,
In every story, loves transcend.
Through time and space, we forge a tie,
In every note, our spirits fly.

So cherish now, this fleeting grace,
In each small moment, time we trace.
An aria sung, our souls afloat,
In letters penned, love's sacred note.

Prelude to a Forgotten World

In twilight's glow, the whispers call,
A world unseen, we knew it all.
Through ancient trees, our footsteps fade,
In realms where memories cascade.

Echoes linger, calling back,
To a place where hearts won't lack.
Lost avenues we long to roam,
In shadows deep, we find our home.

Veils of mist and secrets weave,
In every breath, a chance to believe.
With every dawn, a story told,
Of love's embrace in shades of gold.

Through shifting sands of time we chase,
The remnants of a lost embrace.
In every flutter, hope resides,
A journey shared, where heart abides.

So let us step into the light,
And wander through the endless night.
In this prelude, dreams unfold,
A forgotten world, a tale retold.

Orchestration of the Night

Stars twinkle high, a sparkling light,
Moon whispers secrets, cloaked in night.
Shadows dance softly on silvered ground,
In the cool breeze, tranquility found.

Crickets sing symphonies under the sky,
While the world sleeps, dreams gently sigh.
Each note a journey, each pause a breath,
In the night's embrace, we find our depth.

Waves of silence wash over the glade,
Nature's soft lullaby, lovingly played.
The world stands still, wrapped in a shroud,
In the harmony, we feel proud.

The orchestra swells with a gentle grace,
In every shadow, beauty we trace.
Whispers of peace in the serene dark,
Each heartbeat echoing, a sacred spark.

Colors of a Brighter Tomorrow

Sunrise breaks, painting the sky,
Brushstrokes of hope as daylight draws nigh.
With every hue, dreams take their flight,
The promise of peace fills the light.

Yellow blooms burst in joyous cheer,
Warmth of the sun, banishing fear.
With every new dawn, possibilities grow,
In the garden of life, seeds we sow.

Leaves turn golden, nature's embrace,
Colors so vivid, lighting the space.
Hands joined together, we reach and strive,
In unity and love, we truly thrive.

With laughter and joy, let's paint the scene,
In every heartbeat, a future unseen.
Together we rise, come what may,
In shades of tomorrow, brighten the day.

The Ballet of Boundless Horizons

Waves crash softly on a distant shore,
Whispers of freedom call out for more.
Dancing clouds drift in the azure blue,
In this ballet, a world born anew.

Steps of the earth, rhythm of life,
Graceful movement, easing the strife.
Mountains stand tall, guardians proud,
Guiding us forward, wrapping us, shroud.

With every pirouette, the stars align,
Gliding through dreams, visions entwine.
A tapestry woven with threads of gold,
Stories of courage, waiting to be told.

On horizons broad, we chase the dawn,
Till shadows retreat and night is gone.
With hearts wide open, we embrace the dance,
In the magic of moments, we find our chance.

Crescendo of Chimeras

In the twilight's fog, visions take flight,
Mystical echoes whisper through night.
A dance of the dreams, surreal and grand,
Where shadows and light weave hand in hand.

Chimeras of hopes flicker and glow,
In the depths of the mind, wild rivers flow.
Each thought a symphony, haunting and sweet,
Resonating deeply, where echoes meet.

In the heart of darkness, the pulse of souls,
A crescendo rising, where aspiration rolls.
With every heartbeat, a new tale spun,
In the tapestry bright, we become one.

As dawn approaches, dreams intertwine,
Reality bends, in a dance so fine.
In the quietest moments, the chimeras play,
Guiding our spirits into the day.

Through the Lens of Dreamers

In twilight's glow, where shadows play,
The dreamers drift, they find their way.
With whispered hopes and stars in sight,
They paint the world in colors bright.

A canvas stretched across the night,
Each stroke a wish, a soft delight.
They weave their tales with threads of light,
In realms where sorrows take to flight.

From mountains high to oceans deep,
The dreamers guard the secrets keep.
In every heart, a story sings,
As dawn unfolds its golden wings.

Through every tear and joyful laugh,
They chart the paths, a guiding half.
With every sigh, a spark ignites,
In dreams, they soar to wondrous heights.

So let us join these souls so free,
And dance with fate, eternally.
Through every shadow, every beam,
We'll journey on, through the lens of dream.

The Pulse of a Hidden Universe

In silence deep, where echoes dwell,
A hidden pulse begins to swell.
The stars align, a cosmic tune,
In whispers soft as night's own rune.

Each heartbeat thrums with ancient lore,
A universe behind closed doors.
Unseen worlds, they twist and sway,
In cosmic dance, they find their way.

Through galaxies of bright allure,
The shadows weave a tale obscure.
For every star that lights the night,
A million more remain out of sight.

And in the dark where dreams take flight,
The pulse ignites, a brilliant light.
For those who dare to seek and roam,
Within, they find a boundless home.

So tune your heart to cosmic sound,
Let stardust guide where dreams are found.
In every pulse, a universe,
Awaits the seeker, blessed and cursed.

Notes from a Forgotten Garden

In corners where the wild things grow,
A garden whispers tales from below.
With petals soft and colors bright,
It holds the dreams of day and night.

Each leaf a memory, time's embrace,
In shadows deep, a sacred space.
The flowers dance, a fleeting glance,
With every breeze, they take their chance.

Through tangled vines and mossy stone,
The echoes of lost laughter drone.
Beneath the boughs, the secrets hide,
Where time forgot, but love abides.

From every hue and fragrant bloom,
A story lingers, chasing gloom.
With every seed that finds its home,
The garden breathes, no more alone.

So wander here, where shadows play,
In every flower, find your way.
For in this space, where dreams do mend,
A forgotten garden knows no end.

Weaving Worlds of Wonder

In threads of gold and silver spun,
We weave a tapestry of fun.
With every stitch, a dream is cast,
Creating worlds that hold us fast.

Through valleys deep and mountains wide,
Each tale unfolds, we take the ride.
With every knot, a fate entwined,
In wondrous realms, our hearts aligned.

The fabric hums with life's embrace,
In every color, joy and grace.
With whispers soft, the stories flow,
A vibrant dance, forever glow.

From roots of earth to skies above,
We weave the strands of hope and love.
In each creation, magic wakes,
As woven dreams, the spirit makes.

So gather close, with hearts so full,
Let's spin our wheels, both bright and dull.
In every world of wonder spun,
We find our place, our souls as one.

Chords of the Heart's Yearning

In silence, whispers call to me,
Each note a soft, sweet memory.
Bound by the ties we used to weave,
Love's echo lingers; I believe.

A symphony of hopes and dreams,
Beneath the moon's soft silver beams.
Together still, though miles apart,
We play the chords of the heart's art.

In twilight's gaze, a gentle hum,
Where warmth and solace both become.
With every beat, I'll hold you near,
Your melody, forever clear.

Through storms, our rhythm sways in time,
Each sigh and laugh, a sacred rhyme.
Resounding through the depths of night,
Our song ignites the darkest light.

So let the music rise once more,
From hidden depths, where spirits soar.
Together, we'll renew the spark,
In chords of longing through the dark.

Ballad of the Brimming Day

The sun ascends in golden rays,
A canvas painted, bright displays.
With laughter, children run and play,
They sing the ballad of the day.

Fields bloom with colors, fresh and new,
The skies adorned in brilliant blue.
Time dances on the morning dew,
Alive within each vibrant hue.

Birds serenade the waking morn,
In joyous notes, their hearts are born.
A gentle breeze, a soft caress,
A moment's peace that feels like rest.

As clouds drift lazily, drawn near,
The world awakens, crystal clear.
Every heartbeat sings the praise,
Of life anew in sunny rays.

With evening's touch, the sky ignites,
And twilight hugs the day in lights.
Yet still we cherish every way,
The ballad sung of the brimming day.

Echoing Past the Veil

Shadows dance in whispered tones,
Voices linger, soft as stones.
Through the veil, they call my name,
Ghostly echoes, never tame.

Old memories like mist appear,
In the stillness, loud and clear.
Fleeting dreams, they weave and play,
Lost within the shades of gray.

Each murmur flows like a stream,
Carrying fragments of a dream.
A tapestry of days gone by,
Threads of laughter, tears, and sighs.

Time drifts slowly, yet so fast,
Each moment gone, cannot last.
Yet still, within this sacred space,
Their essence holds a warm embrace.

Through the ethereal, we roam,
In every heart, we find a home.
Echoing softly, they reveal,
The love that lies beyond the veil.

The Alchemy of Nightmares

In shadows deep, where phantoms tread,
Whispers coil around my head.
Night's dark magic, fierce and wild,
Unruly thoughts by fears beguiled.

A twisted dance within my mind,
Fragments of what I left behind.
In dreams, the monsters take their flight,
Forged by darkness, wrapped in night.

Yet in this chaos, I find gold,
Strength from stories left untold.
Each trial shapes the heart anew,
In alchemy of nightmares, true.

There lies a spark, a flickering flame,
Within the depths, I learn my name.
From haunting fears, I rise and fight,
Transforming dread to hopeful light.

So let the shadows come to dance,
For in their grasp, I find my chance.
To turn the dark to something bright,
In alchemy of endless night.

Starlit Contemplations

Beneath the vast and velvet sky,
The stars like dreams begin to sigh.
Each twinkle whispers tales of old,
In night's embrace, their secrets hold.

A gentle breeze caresses the night,
As thoughts take flight on wings of light.
In silence, I ponder the unseen,
In shadows deep, where doubts convene.

The moonlit path guides my wayward heart,
In solitude, where journeys start.
With every star, a wish is born,
A quiet hope, amidst the scorn.

Yet in the stillness, echoes play,
Reminding tales of yesterday.
For every star that lights the dark,
There's a flicker of joy, a tiny spark.

So I sit here with dreams alight,
In starlit contemplations of the night.
Each moment precious, fleeting too,
In the universe, I find my view.

Symphony of the Solitary Soul

In twilight's hush, a whisper flows,
A melody only solitude knows.
Each note composed from silent tears,
A symphony played through the years.

The heartstrings tug, a gentle pull,
In the quiet, the soul feels full.
With every heartbeat, a rhythm found,
In the solitude, a sacred sound.

Alone yet whole, I find my grace,
In vacant spaces, I embrace.
Each chord a reflection of my plight,
A journey walked in the dim light.

The echoes dance in twilight's balm,
Each rising note, a breath of calm.
Though solitude calls, I am not lone,
In this symphony, I find my home.

So here I sit, in shadows deep,
As secrets of the heart I keep.
With every song, I learn to soar,
In the solitude, I long for more.

Odes to the Ethereal

In realms of dreams, where whispers flow,
The ethereal light begins to glow.
With every dawn, a promise made,
In golden hues, my fears will fade.

I wander through the misty air,
Embracing visions, rich and rare.
Each step unfolds a tapestry,
Of life's most vibrant mastery.

The stars align with gentle grace,
In this vast universe, I find my place.
With every breath, the magic sings,
An ode to all the joy it brings.

Amidst the night, I dance with light,
In ethereal warmth, my soul takes flight.
Through dreams and hopes that intertwine,
I rise above, forever shine.

So here I write my heartfelt ode,
To moments lived on this sacred road.
In ethereal realms where spirits soar,
I celebrate life forevermore.

Harmonies of Heartfelt Whispers

In twilight's embrace, soft whispers bloom,
Carried through the night, dispelling gloom.
Each word a note in a tender song,
Harmonies shared where hearts belong.

The gentle rustle of the leaves,
In nature's choir, the spirit grieves.
Yet still, within this sacred space,
The echoes linger, a warm embrace.

A symphony of dreams takes flight,
As starlit skies embrace the night.
Each heartbeat matches the love we find,
In whispers deep, two souls aligned.

With every laugh, a memory spills,
In gentle tones, the heart fulfills.
Harmonies rise, soft and sweet,
In the dance of whispers, we find our beat.

So let the world fade into the night,
In heartfelt whispers, we find our light.
In this symphony of love, we soar,
Forever entwined, forevermore.

Orchestration of Ethereal Fantasies

In twilight's gentle embrace, dreams align,
Whispers of starlight weave through the pine.
Notes of a symphony call from afar,
An echo of magic, a guiding star.

Dancing shadows flicker, alive with grace,
Each moment a canvas, the night an embrace.
Through realms of the unknown, we wander free,
Crafting our stories in reverie.

Waves of soft laughter, a melody sweet,
With every heartbeat, the world feels complete.
Entwined with the cosmos, our spirits arise,
Painting the heavens with luminous skies.

Secrets of galaxies sparkle in view,
Holding the essence of hopes and hues.
Dreams merge with stardust, igniting the dark,
The orchestration of life leaves its mark.

Serenade of wonder, a lullaby's tune,
Echoing softly beneath the bright moon.
In the symphony of night, we find our place,
An orchestration of dreams, a loving embrace.

Interlude of Celestial Hopes

In the silence of night, hope softly sings,
Beneath cosmic blankets, dreams take on wings.
Every twinkling star, a promise so bright,
Guiding our hearts in the dark of the night.

Whispers of wishes drift through the air,
Interwoven tales of love and of care.
Moments of stillness call out our names,
While our souls ignite in celestial flames.

Carried on stardust, we traverse the skies,
In a realm where the magic of longing lies.
Every heartbeat echoes a truth we seek,
In the interlude's grace, we find what we speak.

Silhouettes of dreams, like clouds in the blue,
We dance with the shadows, embracing the new.
In this fleeting pause, we savor the glow,
Of celestial hopes that forever will flow.

With each dawn that breaks, a promise appears,
In the interlude's warmth, we shed our fears.
Holding on tightly to visions that gleam,
Together we'll wander, forever we'll dream.

Tapestry of Somnolent Adventures

In fields of slumber, dreams gently tread,
Sailing on clouds, where the wild thoughts spread.
Each thread of the night, a story untold,
In patterns of wonder, in whispers of gold.

Waves of tranquility envelop our hearts,
In slumber's embrace, true freedom imparts.
Mirrored reflections of who we might be,
In this tapestry woven with wild reverie.

Drifting through landscapes, both strange and divine,
With eyes wide shut, we dance through the time.
Twilit horizons, where fantasies brew,
In the fabric of night, we craft something new.

Echoes of laughter float softly around,
In the silence of dreams, our solace is found.
Adventures await in the depths of our sleep,
A tapestry vibrant, our secrets to keep.

Awaken, dear dreamer, the dawn's glowing ray,
Invites us to savor the honeyed ballet.
In the tapestry spun, as our spirits take flight,
Adventures of slumber persist in the light.

Overture of Boundless Possibilities

In the dawn's soft glow, life stretches and yawns,
The overture beckons, a symphony dawns.
With every new moment, a chance to embrace,
The layout of futures, of hope's warm face.

Fields of desires bloom vast in our minds,
We dance with the echoes that fate often binds.
Wings of ambitions unfold with each breath,
In the overture's pulse, we rise from our depth.

A canvas before us, painted with dreams,
Whispers of fortune flow like silver streams.
In harmony's embrace, we find our own way,
The symphony calls, as we seize the day.

Mirrors reflect visions of life yet to come,
In a world full of wonders, we gallantly hum.
With every heartbeat, the music takes flight,
The overture sings, promising light.

With spirits unbound, we'll chase the unknown,
In the heart of the moment, we find our true home.
An overture of life, with endless reprieve,
In the dance of existence, we learn how to believe.

Chasing Dreams Across Time

In the dawn's gentle light, we start,
Each dream a whisper, a beating heart.
We chase the shadows that dance in the mist,
Timeless adventures, not to be missed.

With every heartbeat, the past comes alive,
We soar through the moments, fiercely we strive.
In echoes of laughter, we find our way,
Chasing these dreams, we greet the day.

Through valleys and mountains, the journey unfolds,
Stories of courage, and legends untold.
The colors of memory paint skies so vast,
Chasing the visions of future and past.

When twilight beckons, and stars begin to gleam,
We ponder the paths we thought to redeem.
In the tapestry woven, our hopes intertwine,
Chasing these dreams, forever they shine.

With every sunrise, new dreams we will chase,
In the fabric of time, we find our place.
Our spirits are free, like birds in the sky,
Chasing these dreams, we learn how to fly.

The Rhythm of Head in Clouds

Floating on whispers of a soft summer breeze,
Thoughts intertwine like the leaves on the trees.
In daydreams we wander, unfurling our wings,
Lost in the music that imagination brings.

With eyes turned to heavens, we drift and we sway,
The rhythm of clouds carries us away.
We dance with the shadows, the sun's golden glow,
In the palace of dreams, where our spirits flow.

As laughter erupts in a symphony sweet,
We find harmony beneath our own feet.
Each heart is a drum, each breath is a note,
In this world of wonders, together we float.

When twilight approaches, and colors ignite,
We gather our thoughts, like stars in the night.
With the rhythm of heartbeats, we're never alone,
In the clouds, we find a place to call home.

Embracing the magic that life loves to weave,
With heads in the clouds, we learn to believe.
The melody lingers, a soft lullaby,
With the rhythm of dreams, we soar through the sky.

Strings of Introspection

In the silence of thought, I trace each line,
Connecting the moments, your heart next to mine.
The strings of reflection, they pull and they sway,
Unraveling stories we weave every day.

A tapestry formed from the threads of our past,
We ponder the shadows, the light that we cast.
With each gentle pluck, a memory sings,
The symphony begs for the truth that it brings.

In corners of quiet, we gather our dreams,
The music of solace flows softly in streams.
Each note is a whisper, a longing, a plea,
The strings of introspection reveal what we see.

As stars start to twinkle, we share our desires,
The warmth of connection ignites hidden fires.
We delve into futures, the paths that we choose,
In the strings of our souls, there's nothing to lose.

Through echoes of kindness, we heal and we grow,
In the journey of introspection, we learn to let go.
With each heartfelt lesson, we rise and we stand,
In the symphony of life, we create hand in hand.

Meditations on Twilight's Edge

At the twilight's edge, the colors collide,
Crimson and gold where the daylight resides.
A moment of pause, in the soft fading light,
We gather our thoughts, embracing the night.

The whispers of dusk bring a calm to our hearts,
As shadows emerge, the stillness imparts.
Each breath is a mantra, a gentle embrace,
In the twilight's glow, we find our own space.

With the stars as our counselors, we gaze to the sky,
In the silence of twilight, all worries pass by.
We ponder the questions that linger inside,
In meditations on twilight, our truths cannot hide.

As the moon takes its throne, the world shifts anew,
We ponder our dreams, the old and the true.
Each heartbeat a rhythm, each thought a soft sigh,
In the evening's embrace, we learn how to fly.

So let us reflect on this fragile descent,
With the twilight as guide, we savor the lent.
In stillness we gather, in peace we release,
At twilight's edge, we discover our peace.

The Palette of Fantasia

In colors bold, the canvas sings,
A world reborn with vibrant springs.
Brushstrokes dance on twilight's edge,
Where dreams entwine at magic's pledge.

Waves of azure, whispers of gold,
Stories woven, ages old.
The heart beats gentle, rhythm so fine,
In every hue, our hopes align.

Soft pastels in the morning light,
Merge with shadows of starry night.
A journey painted with every sigh,
Through valleys deep and mountains high.

Clouds of lavender drift and soar,
In this realm where spirits explore.
With each stroke, a tale unfolds,
In the palette of dreams, the bold.

Crimson roses cling to time,
Their fragrance lingers, pure, sublime.
As whispers echo through the glade,
In the garden of dreams, love is made.

Lyrical Visions

In whispers soft, the verses flow,
A tapestry where feelings grow.
Starlit nights where secrets weave,
With every word, our hearts believe.

Melodies dance on twilight's breeze,
Carrying tales like rustling leaves.
In shadows deep, the light will gleam,
Awakening the lost, the dream.

Each line a window, each rhyme a door,
To realms where spirits leap and soar.
With every stanza, bright worlds awake,
In lyrical visions, we heartily stake.

The moonlight bathes the silent ground,
In this refuge where peace is found.
As thoughts take flight on wings of grace,
In this lyrical love, we find our place.

Time stands still, as feelings merge,
In harmony, we feel the surge.
With soft refrains, our souls align,
In the symphony of the divine.

Dreamscapes Unraveled

In dreamscapes vast, we wander free,
Unraveling tales of what can be.
A tapestry spun with silver threads,
Whispers of wonders in twilight spreads.

Stars like lanterns guide our way,
Illuminating night from day.
With each step forward, visions bloom,
In this realm of midnight's loom.

The mountains breathe with stories untold,
As the rivers shimmer in liquid gold.
A canvas painted with passion's fire,
In dreamscapes, we reach ever higher.

Gentle echoes of laughter ring,
As time stops still, we start to sing.
In shadows deep, our spirits twine,
In this enchanted land, we redefine.

Through misty valleys, we chase the light,
Awakening dreams, igniting the night.
As realities blur and edges fade,
In dreamscapes unraveled, love is made.

Spheres of the Ethereal

In spheres of light, we drift and glide,
Beyond the veil where secrets hide.
Echoes of whispers, soft as a sigh,
In the ethereal dance, we learn to fly.

Celestial spirits weave through air,
On wings of hope, they gently care.
With every heartbeat, the universe sings,
In this realm of magic, love takes wing.

Galaxies twirl in a cosmic embrace,
As stardust weaves through time and space.
In every moment, the beauty grows,
In spheres unseen, our spirit flows.

The dreams we hold take flight at dawn,
Painting horizons as shadows yawn.
With each breath, we find our way,
In this ethereal night's ballet.

With cosmic grace, we rise anew,
In the spheres where grace shines through.
As love encircles, our hearts ignite,
In the realm of the ethereal light.

www.ingramcontent.com/pod-product-compliance
Lightning Source LLC
LaVergne TN
LVHW050012050125
800368LV00017B/168